CHAIRMANIA

CHAIRMANIA

FANTASTIC MINIATURES

GEORGE M. BEYLERIAN

Text by David McFadden
Foreword by Rita Reif

Photography by Ilisa Katz

Harry N. Abrams, Inc., Publishers

Editor:
Ruth A. Peltason

Art Director:
Samuel N. Antupit

Page 2:
Nick Agid
United States
CHAIRS OF CHAIR. 1991
Granite, concrete, wood, brick
6 x 2½ x 3½"

Page 5:
Hans Wegner
Denmark
RING CHAIR. 1955
Wood, cord, cotton
7¾ x 8¾ x 6½"

Front cover: See page 39

Back cover: See page 73

Library of Congress Cataloging-in-Publication

Beylerian, George M.
Chairmania: fantastic miniatures / by
George M Beylerian; text by David
McFadden; foreword by Rita Reif.
p. cm.
ISBN 0–8109–3193–1
1. Miniature chairs—Private
collections—United States—Catalogs.
2. Beylerian, George M.—Art
collections—Catalogs. I. McFadden,
David Revere. II. Title. III. Title:
Chairmania.
NK2715.B49 1994
749'.32'0228—dc20   94–1546

Published in 1994 by Harry N. Abrams,
Incorporated, New York
A Times Mirror Company

Printed and bound in Hong Kong

CONTENTS

FOREWORD

by Rita Reif

Chairs comfort and confound us. Womblike or as lethal looking as meshed twigs, they were conceived to replace the laps we knew in infancy. While we depend on chairs to ease our aches, cradle our spines, rest our arms, and improve our temperaments, rarely are we satisfied for long with the artifacts on which we sit. Gut instincts are supposed to tell us what suits us best. And so we go on seeking the ideal chair, the one that looks right, feels right, and will last forever.

On finding what we think is our dream chair, however, we tend to be ungracious, focusing quickly on its faults. The seat is too hard, too soft, too low or too high. The back is too straight or too angled. And there are no wings. The legs? Straight ones produce cramps when you wrap your feet around them. Raked ones trip you up. Cabrioles with claws are too curvy for comfort. Tripods may be better—especially those with wheels, providing surfaces on which to rest one's feet. But rolling chairs are not perfect either—uncontrollable on smooth floors, suicidal where there's a slant.

Anyway, who ever heard of a Windsor on wheels with wings?

If it does exist, George Beylerian will find it, especially if it comes as a miniature. Beylerian has been involved in the business of chairs for more than thirty years—as a merchant, a manufacturer, a design consultant, and, most recently, as a collector of miniatures. A restless spirit, this mensch is also an optimist with an insatiable appetite. Beylerian decided to experience as many chairs as possible, made throughout history, by finding hundreds of them in tiny versions.

With this as his agenda, chairs became a treat instead of a test. Who knew or much less cared about such practical concerns as whether the frames wobbled, the legs wiggled, or the casters squeaked. In Valhalla, after all, the gods' recliners are upholstered in clouds. Perfection was possible, indeed probable, he reckoned, in a world where fantasy ruled and everything was no more than ten inches tall. He determined he would specialize in miniatures possessing a monumental presence.

And so he began his pursuit of the offbeat and outrageous in pint-sized seats. Since thinking small has never been Beylerian's style, he gave in to his collecting avocation six years ago when he went on a worldwide chair-buying spree. He let his keen eye, obsessive nature, and gargantuan appetite guide him as he swept through shopping malls, antiques shows, crafts fairs, and giant flea markets on five continents. And he became, for a time, a Medici to the makers of miniatures, commissioning artists, artisans, and architects in New York, Milan, Paris, Copenhagen, Santa Fe, and Oaxaca to produce the grandest or goofiest fantasy chairs, each sized to carry away in his pocket.

As it turned out—and as reflected in this book—esoteric chairs in offbeat materials, forms, and decoration outnumbered the classics in the marketplace. Certainly there were tiny examples of Charles Rennie Mackintosh's tearoom ladderback chairs, Ludwig Mies van der Rohe's tubular steel Bauhaus chairs, Gerrit Rietveld's Red-Blue chairs, and Charles Eames's plastic shells on legs, all of which Beylerian bought.

But these designers, and Thomas Chippendale before them, never considered constructing chairs in the way, for example, Neal Small did in the 1990s, using only a bunch of brushes in one case, a matchbook in another. For that matter, Georges Jacob, a master *menuisier* of the eighteenth century, also had no sense of humor. After surviving his royal patrons, Marie Antoinette and Louis XVI, Jacob created chairs for Napoleon and Josephine to sit on at Malmaison, but he lacked the wit to devise the chair to end all chairs, based on the historically defining object of his day. That came two hundred years later when Dragoslav Scepanovic, an American from Yugoslavia, created the guillotine chair, a fitting ending for Beylerian's seating saga.

Once Beylerian had reviewed the world of chairs and collected twice the number shown on these pages, their history seemed more comprehensible. Chairs have been around for almost as long as folks have been sitting. The first human being to need a chair may well have been a power-conscious type, someone, perhaps, smart enough to perceive a political advantage in achieving additional height. No one knows when thrones appeared. But they were probably in use by the Stone Age. Rocks could have functioned as royal seats in the neolithic period, appealing to the dual-purpose instincts of Neanderthals who would have known best what great weapons boulders were.

As far as we know, chairs of wood were an Egyptian invention some four thousand years ago. Less than five hundred years later, chairs were so popular throughout the ancient world that the Mycenaeans of early Greece decided to take them to their graves in the form of pottery miniatures.

Beylerian, an Armenian-American born in Egypt, has traveled widely throughout the Mediterranean, exploring tomb furnishings as he went. While no one knows whether these clay chairs were created in antiquity as toys or as collectibles, they offer clues to the sort of items valued then as status symbols; today, thousands of years later, they pique our fancy and intrigue us.

There's also this matter of scale that is seductive. Somehow chairs at one-fifth their normal size invariably seem, if not always beautiful, then at least innocent and far more inviting than many full-scale models. We tolerate the excesses of decoration on just about any chair that fits in the palm of one hand. At Lilliputian scale, even the elaborately carved dark wood chairs in a Renaissance palace and the lavishly gilded seating at Versailles are seductive and not one bit unbearable. And we marvel at the skills of the makers of these objects, who bedazzle us with their complex forms.

Miniatures became serious business in eighteenth-century Europe as the middle class burgeoned and furniture styles proliferated. Chair makers traveled from town to town, taking along scaled-down samples of chairs to spur orders, while other producers devised models to be shown at their shops to clients. Dollhouses, in existence since at least the seventeenth century, were mass-produced two hundred years later in Europe and the United States. The chairs furnishing these dwellings from cellar to attic were as bourgeois as the full-scale originals.

While the vast majority of chairs by twentieth-century architects and industrial designers exist in diminutive form, realism is less pervasive in the late twentieth-century miniatures. In fact, most of the chairs on the following pages do not exist as real chairs at all. Delightfully unconventional, even audacious in their sumptuous decoration, many combine a sense of wit and surrealism that are absent in most of the seats we sit on today.

The world may have millions—billions—of chairs. But there's always room on Earth for more—especially since most of us are still looking for the one that looks better, works better, or just makes us smile.

INTRODUCTION

Collectors have been described as driven and insecure, obsessed, greedy, and compulsive. This does not, however, make them "bad" people—but they are very, very determined people. Once a collector latches onto an idea, pursuit and the impact of an accumulation of objects become paramount. Impact is necessary for bringing attention or awareness to an idea, visually and conceptually.

In the case of Chairmania, the main idea behind the years of collecting miniature chairs has been my interest in exploring the tremendous variations in the design of a chair. The diversity of materials used, the design techniques, and the function of the chair all add to the richness of this collection.

In Chairmania these variations are particularly emphasized because of the miniature scale in which they have been created. It is easier to fantasize in a highly reduced scale, whereas space and volume would otherwise deter the actual production of so many outlandish interpretations.

The Chairmania collection presented in this book has been generally labeled as one that evolves around the notion of *fantasy,* even though some of the pieces shown here are miniature versions of chairs that at one time or another actually have been produced full size. But consider: Who would dare make a full-scale chair that was entirely beaded, or constructed of theater tickets, or of forks and knives, or even of wheat stalks? An ingenious folk artist, or someone with a demanding cigarette habit, or perhaps just someone with a lot of idle time decided to create a miniature chair by braiding empty cigarette wrappers; one artist used a doily to wrap around a chair frame, and yet another artist used Tabasco bottles and scouring pads.

When it comes to collecting almost anything, the first hint of a mania comes by way of some chemical reaction in one's brain. Maybe there is some great challenge at hand (such as someone else's collection!), or maybe another collection inspires or sets off an idea; maybe there just is some personal association with the objects being collected. Whatever the motivation, the germ of any would-be collector is usually there all along until some happening triggers what I think of as the "challenge button."

Once pressed, a euphoric and compulsive wave sets in, and there's no stopping until "quantities" of objects are amassed to establish the new collection. This is the "counting" stage when one can immediately say how many pieces are in the collection. At this early stage, purchases or additions tend to be indiscriminate.

Needless to say, certain parameters must be set if the collector has any dignity. Such parameters could focus on style, price, origin. In the case of Chairmania, size is obviously the ruling criterion. My very first chair, and the first one in this book, was given to me as a trade promotion gift during a trip to Udine, Italy—the chair manufacturing capital of the world. This classic country chair sat on a shelf at my beach house for a few years when one day I noticed in a curio shop in the village a twig love seat which I bought on impulse. It too sat on the same shelf for a while. It had not yet occurred to me that I was "catching a bug." Still, in complete innocence, I accumulated two or three more chairs, until I realized that my good friend Dorothy Kalins had just a few more chairs than me.

As a former producer of real-life chairs I suddenly realized that first, I had an affinity with chairs, and that second, there were actually more miniature chairs than I was ever aware of. But where, what, how?

That's when the "chemical reaction" took place somewhere in my head, and the race began.

This chemical reaction gave me an excuse to enter any shop, antique or otherwise, in the pursuit of my new hobby, and for the sake of spotting a chair or two. And indeed they were to be found. Whereas before I had never seen or noticed even one miniature chair, now I found that they were in abundant supply. Each find—good or bad—brought along a sense of great fulfillment.

Flea markets are obviously a place of great adventure. One should remain focused and slick at spotting objects, all the while moving swiftly in order to cover a lot of ground. A pair of additional eyes helps along the way. One of the most joyful days of my life was the unforgettable trip to Brimfield, Massachusetts, *the* flea market event of the East Coast.

Antonio Morello and Donato Savoie joined me and my wife, Louise, at dawn at a traditional Fourth of July Brimfield market. Having spent the night in a nearby motel, we were able to be at the right place and at the right time: 5 A.M.

Antonio went around to every exhibitor asking if they had "little chairs," explaining his request in minute detail. I suggested to him that his method was taking up too much time and that it was much faster and more efficient to just look. If a vendor had little chairs, they'd be out there in the open. The catch of that day amounted to thirty-six chairs! The large, soft bag I had brought along got emptied twice into the trunk of my station wagon.

This was truly an exhilarating experience and pushed me into the category of the "serious collector." There was no stopping at this point. Soon I was numbering and documenting each piece in an archival system of my own design.

Months later, as I scanned a pier show, I discovered a salesman's sample (which are always miniature in size), but alas, with a hefty price tag. The dealer sympathized with my agony. Her advice was to sell some of my "lesser, previously acquired pieces" (obviously not of great quality) and convert the proceeds to a true "collector's piece." How could she even suggest that I get rid of my lovingly collected pieces? Many chairs later, indeed some of the early pieces were deaccessioned. They were not sold as she suggested—they were simply removed to a shelf or two in the storage room. By then I had lost easy count of the collection. It was no longer a question of bragging about "how many chairs in the collection." A certain attitude evolved, which continues to this date: Numbers are no longer important, but matters of quality, individuality, and originality are what really "count." Nor is it always the most extravagant chairs that are prized. Many unpretentious miniatures have a soul of their own either in their funkiness, sensitivity, or in their utter simplicity—like the twine chair made by a Navajo man during an impromptu encounter with Sevan Melikyan, who worked as my assistant at the time.

One aspect of collecting that is most gratifying is the discipline that one eventually develops. One gets to feel professional at it—one even learns to turn down opportunities. Another rewarding aspect of collecting is the occasional discovery of bargains. There's no great fun paying full price for a new find; the moment of gratification comes when the seller asks for a ridiculously low price and you know you're getting a great bargain. For example, this is how I bought my favorite "Lifeguard" chair for only $10. It had taken me all of two minutes to stop at the dealer's stand in Brimfield and complete the transaction. I like to think that dealer has been blessed for having given me such a good buy.

And then there are the friends who have helped with the collection, and indeed they are a true support group. They seem to want to "join the team" and be part of the addiction. I have acknowledged all my beautiful friends, relatives, and fellow collectors who have generously helped me in building up the collection. My friend Maynard Hale Lyndon has singly spotted and purchased some of my prize pieces. He has also created and made some chairs for me. Our relationship over the past two years or so has produced a file of at least sixty pieces of delightful correspondence, which is an important part of the collection. He and his wife, Lu, have visited us from Boston frequently to keep an eye on the collection and to check which categories have needed reinforcements.

My wife, Louise, who hates possessions, collections, and accumulations, has been most generous in the process. Not only did she contribute some of the best pieces to the collection, she has, most of all, allowed the collection to take over the most usable spaces of our household—usable spaces such as the buffet serving area and the guest room—until we converted one end of our house into a tiny museum containing at least four hundred chairs! I think she secretly loves my adopted children and shows them off when I'm not around.

Our children have also managed to offer major contributions: my son Gregory made my favorite two pieces in the collection—not an easy challenge! And my daughter Carina, in her typical communicative style, came up with *Chairmania,* the name for my chair collecting passion.

Very close friends, like Zimmie Sasson, turned out to be my devoted international eyes and ears. Zimmie found chairs for me in the open markets of Siena and in the finest antique dealers' shops in London. Her passion seems to equal mine. Evelyn Farland insisted that I get the Christian Dior miniature Louis XVI bergère, a promotional object for Dior eyewear that could be found only in opticians' windows. She wouldn't give up until she managed to get one for my collection from her optician.

Other intimate friends, among them Neal Small, plunged into the mania and helped to produce a torrent of collectibles. Neal's creations appear in the gatefold of the Transformer section of this book. Wit and originality—in terms of materials, shapes, and textures—make them outlandish and very amusing. There's obviously something infectious about collecting that grabs people when a sympathetic idea comes about. In the case of Neal Small, it was the collector triggering the passion in the artist. (I later found out that my friend Small was obsessed by small chairs.)

And then there are the believers who heard about the collection and felt strongly enough about it to create a chair and present it to Chairmania as a loan or gift. There are those who, like me, got the bug. My friend and great artist Robert Ebendorf made two of the most splendid pieces in the collection and, like the Pied Piper, brought along other artist friends. Ebendorf was inspired to actually produce a miniature chair collection for a show in his L.A. gallery, which he called "Homage to Mr. Chairmania."

Finally, there are the wannabes, the late arrivals, who see where things have come to, and absolutely want to be part of the scene. Some ingenious additions that are obviously "different" from any other pieces in the collection have come this way. During my recent years organizing exhibitions as curator or producer, I've experienced many late entries in invitational exhibits. These late entries are always welcome as a "bonus," because one has given up hope on getting them.

Today, the collection has reached vast proportions and promises to continue to grow. This book presents some of the most dramatic examples of miniature chairs in each of the categories which we created. Needless to say, a chair will often fall into more than one category. In these cases, the most distinctive characteristic of the chair was used as the criterion for assigning it the most appropriate category. Artists, craftsmen, architects, product designers have all been considered as equal creators.

Chairmania has a broader purpose than simply to celebrate the "oeuvres de maitre" of yesteryear up to the present: It also includes folk art, some of it naive, some of it sophisticated in its own way. Other chairs display tribal and ethnic influences. Many display the ingenuity of some creative spirit who has been able to put a great deal of mastery and power into the concept of the chair. Symbolism in chair design goes a long way. For this reason the book ends with the category "Seats of Power."

Finally, I thought that since we had every kind of chair—including the wheelchair created by Gregory Beylerian and suggested by David McFadden—I needed a guillotine chair to end this book. This little terror would be the ultimate executioner of evil miniature chairs. After all, why shouldn't miniature life mimic real life?

For all the pleasures that have gone into making this book about Chairmania, I want to acknowledge Rita Reif and David McFadden, who contributed their creative talents to formulate categories that were most expressive of the collection. Furthermore, they have graciously contributed their words of wisdom to this book, for which I thank them.

I wish to thank the three collaborators who have succeeded each other in the development process of Chairmania: Sevan Melikyan and Linda Ganjian, my initial curatorial assistants, followed by Kevin Murphy, who has been collaborating on the project in different roles and with great dedication and care. Trudi Smith has organized all the written material for the computer in record time!

I thank my editor Ruth Peltason at Harry N. Abrams, Inc., for taking a firm stand on all the details pertaining to this beautiful book and for her vision, together with Paul Gottlieb's, for having so much faith in this project. A special thanks goes to Sam Antupit, who, with his inimitable kindness, has directed our collaboration with the fabulous photography of Ilisa Katz.

George M. Beylerian
January 1994

Miniature furniture has delighted and charmed adults (as well as children) in seventeenth-century aristocratic households, in nineteenth-century nurseries, and in the homes and offices of today's collectors. When the term *miniature*—used to describe any object made in a highly reduced scale—is applied to furniture, it suggests a world in which fantasy and imagination triumph over practical function in the real world.

Within the field of miniature furniture, chairs seem to have always held pride of place among designers and artisans and among most collectors. Certainly more chairs seem to have survived than other furniture forms, suggesting that the form was a favorite in the past as well as in the present. Taken as a group, however, these diminutive seats raise a fundamental question: other than providing a lively field for modern collectors, why were so many of these "useless" reminders of daily life actually made? While the visual delight and amusement of their original owners is undoubtedly the foundation stone upon which the genre developed, other functions and purposes have been addressed in Lilliputian design. As with any class of collectible, romantic legends abound, one claiming that miniatures were used as salesmen's samples and carried from village to village by itinerant artisans. Another theory holds that small chairs may have been submitted as virtuoso works by ambitious and talented apprentices in furniture workshops. While these attractive uses remain tantalizing possibilities, they are not generally accepted, nor are they well documented.

18

In our modern century of mass marketing and commercial promotion, by contrast, the furniture industry has actually created a new category of collectibles in the form of advertising or promotional miniatures that faithfully reproduce (and remind us) of their products. Like an antique salesman's sample, these small mementos describe the form and materials of a chair and alert potential buyers to their availability. Salesmanship and marketing goals in fields quite unrelated to seating are also addressed by small chairs: miniature furniture has been used to promote and advertise a wide variety of consumer goods that ranges from eyeglasses to shoes!

Other functions admirably addressed by small seats include the disguised storage of other (and often unrelated) small items: some chairs offer a secret cache for women's (or men's) jewelry, for buttons or bibelots. Not surprisingly, pairs of chairs—usually matching—have been called into table service as salt and pepper dispensers. Key chains and sewing pins, pipes and other smoking paraphernalia have all been offered a resting place in miniature chairs.

Stretching the envelope of kitsch are miniature chairs sold as souvenirs of visits, often to extraordinarily ordinary places. These functionless chairs, which seem like such appropriate reminders of pleasurable times, have the tendency to occupy the hidden areas of cupboards and drawers for years after the event. Each of these promoters and pretenders proves that business and pleasure can indeed sit comfortably together in a miniature chair.

Left to right:
Handcrafted by La Furlana
Italy
MY FIRST CHAIR. 1988
Wood, rush seat
8¼ x 3½ x 3⅛"

Cini Boeri for Arflex
United States
**STRIPS LOUNGE
CHAIR.**
20th century
Cotton fabric, zipper
6½ x 8 x 8"

Michael Shields for
Brayton International
United States
HOLLIS. 1991
Leather, wood
8¾ x 6½ x 4¾"

20

21

Left to right:
Aldo Cibic for Standard
Italy (b. United States)
SALESMAN'S SAMPLE:
SA 09. 1991
Painted wood to mimic the
original metal design
7 x 3 x 3½"

Spain
ARNE JACOBSEN
IMITATION
SWAN CHAIR.
20th century
Plastic, metal
2½ x 2¼ x 2"

France
STACKING
CHAIR.
20th century
Plastic
3¾ x 2½ x 2½"

Dhana Solish
United States
L.A.
ARCHETYPE
SERIES—
CHINESE
THEATER
CHAIR. 1993
Wood
12⅛ x 4½ x 4½"

Left to right:
Anna Castelli Ferrieri
for Kartell
Italy
STACKING CHAIR. 1985
Plastic
2¾ x 1¾ x 1¾"

Pascal Mourgue
for Fermob
France
LUNE D'ARGENT. 1984
Metal
6 x 4½ x 3½"

Verner Panton for Vitra
Germany
PANTON CHAIRS. 1992
(original design 1967)
Plastic
3⅛ x 2 x 2"

23

Manufactured by Stow Davis
Furniture
United States
**SALESMEN'S SAMPLE:
ARM SWIVEL CHAIR
FROM THE "ADAM"
SUITE.** 1915–39
Leather, wood, metal
9 x 7¼ x 7¼" (one-quarter
scale model)

24

Manufactured by
Weatherend™ Estate Furniture
United States
**SALESMAN'S SAMPLE:
DARK HARBOR®
ROCKING CHAIR AND
CARRY CASE.** 1985
High-gloss white Awlgrip®
painted over mahogany
10 x 6 x 8¼"

United States
SALESMAN'S SAMPLE:
PATIO CHAISE LOUNGE.
c. 1940s
Metal, vinyl
9½ x 15½ x 7½″

26

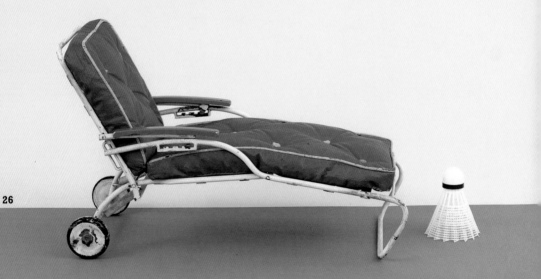

Dorothy Bauer/Piece of the
Rainbow
United States
CHAIR PURSE (seat hinged
with storage under seat).
1992
Swarovski crystals, gold plate
11⅛ x 4½ x 5″

Small chair on top:
SODA FOUNTAIN CHAIR.
1990
Swarovski crystals, gold plate
3½ x 1½ x 1″

Left to right:

Taiwan
KEY CHAIN CHAIR. 1992
Plastic
3 x 2 x 1½″

United States
PIPE HOLDER CHAIR.
c. 1950
Resin
2½ x 3 x 3¼″

China
SOFA JEWELRY BOX
(hinged; seat and back lift
up). 1991
Silver plate
2¾ x 4¾ x 3″

United States
TRINKET CHAIR (storage
compartment under seat).
20th century
Fabric
5 x 3¾ x 3½″

France
**LOUIS XV–STYLE
BERGÈRE** (storage compart-
ment under seat). c. 1920
Wood, fabric
6½ x 4 x 3″

Mexico
TREASURE CHAIR (stor-
age compartment under seat).
20th century
Leather, wood
5 x 5 x 4″

Left to right:

Japan for U.S. market

TEEN-RIFFIC SODA FOUNTAIN CHAIR (EAR-RING HOLDER). 1967

Painted steel, lacquered wood

9 x 2½ x 2½"

United States

NATURAL BRIDGE, VIRGINIA SALT & PEPPER SHAKER CHAIRS. 20th century

Wire, ceramic

4½ x 2½ x 2½"

Japan

VICTORIAN-STYLE OVERSTUFFED SALT SHAKER. c. 1950

Porcelain

2½ x 2½ x 2"

29

United States

CHAIR AND SOFA SALT & PEPPER SHAKERS.

20th century

Ceramic

Chair: 1¾ x 1½ x 1½"

Sofa: 1¾ x 2¼ x 1½"

United States

SALT & PEPPER SHAKER CHAIRS.

20th century

Cast metal

2¼ x 1½ x 2"

Left to right:
United States
SEWING KIT CHAIR.
c. 1920
Fabric, pom-pom fringe
12 x 7½ x 7¾"

United States
**RALPH WALDO
EMERSON CHAIR.** 1990
Wood, metal, battery
9¾ x 4½ x 5"

United States
**LOUIS XV–STYLE
FAUTEUIL TREE
ORNAMENT CHAIR.** 1990
Painted wood, fabric
4¼ x 3 x 3"

Helen D.
United States
**LOUIS XVI–STYLE
FAUTEUIL.** 1981
Ceramic
2¾ x 2 x 2"

30

Left to right:

Taiwan
TREE ORNAMENT
LOVESEAT. 20th century
Wood, cane
3 x 4½ x 2″

United States
SEWING CHAIR (storage
compartment under seat).
c. 1930
Cotton fabric
8¾ x 4¼ x 5¼″

United States
SEWING ROCKER. Early
20th century
Wood, brocade fabric
10½ x 9 x 9¾″

31

France
SALT DISPENSER
CHAIR. c. 1915
Wood
8 x 5 x 5"

Left to right:
United States
BAD AXE, MICHIGAN
SOUVENIR. 1930
Tree trunk
5½ x 2½ x 2½"

Colombia
KEY CHAIN PEN WITH
ASHTRAY CHAIR. 1991
Wood, metal
5¼ x 3½ x 3½"

Spain
BARCELONA ASHTRAY
CHAIR. 1990
Damascene brass
4 x 4 x 2½"

Colombia
ASHTRAY CHAIR. 1991
Wood, metal
3¾ x 3¾ x 3¾"

33

Left to right:
Garouste & Bonetti for Neotu
France
**PROMOTION FOR NYC
NEOTU GALLERY
OPENING.** 1989 (original
chair design 1985)
Painted lead
2 x ¾ x ¾"

France
**CHRISTIAN DIOR
PROMOTION CHAIR—
LOUIS XVI–STYLE.**
c. 1985
Wood, velvet
13¼ x 6½ x 6"

United States
**OWI PROMOTION
CHAIR
FOR SHOES.** 1993
Wood, plastic
3 x 1½ x 2¾"

Denmark
**LYDOLFF PROMOTION
CHAIR—FOLDING
PHONE BOOK CHAIR.**
20th century
Plastic
4½ x 3 x 6¼"

United States
**CHAIRY-TOY CHAIR
FROM PEE WEE'S
PLAYHOUSE.** 1988
Flocked plastic
4 x 3 x 2½″

Sylvia Netzer
United States
**PEDESTAL TEDDY BEAR
CHAIR.** 1993
Teddy bears
7 x 3½ x 4″

United States
PUZZLE ROCKER. c. 1920
Wood
3¾ x 2 x 5″

AMERICANA

Miniature furniture was made in America at least as early as the eighteenth century, although only a comparative handful of pieces from this early period survive and are prized rarities. Those few that are extant have most often entered the collections of museums or distinguished private collections. More miniature furniture made in America survives from the nineteenth century, when the spririt of American invention was in the air. Scores of superb small models of innovative chairs and other seating designs, made between 1836 and 1880, were submitted to the U.S. Patent Office.

Contiguous in time with pedigreed miniature chairs registered with the patent office were a myriad of other miniatures made for the delectation of children and adults throughout the country. And in our own century, legendary collectors and collection-builders have further stimulated the design and production of small chairs. Consider, for example, Mrs. Oakley Thorne of Chicago, whose well-publicized and exceptionally popular miniature rooms, each furnished with detailed and accurate versions of full-scale furniture and room interiors, further dignified the status of the period-style miniature American chairs.

During the eighteenth century, a recognizably American style had flowered in the colonies, displaying a wide variety of distinctive regional accents. Miniature chairs with turned or carved legs and backs were made throughout New England, but so too were elegant carved side and armchairs with impressive claw-and-ball feet. Typically American miniature chairs made from the eighteenth century onward included the Windsor-type chair. Originally inspired by English

Windsor–type chairs made in large numbers during the eighteenth century, the Windsor took on special meaning in American homes. The elegant silhouette of this chair was created by a series of linear uprights that supported the back or arms. These uprights were mortised into a solid seat, which was often carved into graceful and comfortable bottom-fitting curves. Windsor-type chairs in miniature have appeared as sturdy side chairs, benches, high stools, and as high-backed chairs with elegant combs.

Rustic chairs identified with specific regional traditions are also known in miniature, such as in Adirondack-type chairs from New York State. These delightful reminders of summer cabins and restful evenings on front porches were lovingly crafted, and sometimes painted, by artisans working in indigenous woods. A more suburban note is sounded in the ubiquitous cantilevered, molded-metal garden chair that has accommodated many a weekend gardener in repose, or the so-called bistro chair of twisted metal. Often, these small wonders display an unrepentant Americanism in the use of the U.S. flag as a decorative motif.

United States
GARDEN CHAIR.
20th century
Painted metal
10 x 7 x 7"

38

Left to right:
James Hastrich & Pierre
Wallack
United States
**COPY OF A FAN-BACK
WINDSOR HIGH CHAIR.**
1993 (original design c. 1780)
Cedar, basswood
6½ x 3¼ x 3½"

United States
**COPY OF A WINDSOR-
BACK CHAIR.** 1991
Wood
13½ x 8 x 6½"

Left to right:
United States
AMERICAN CHAIR.
c. 1980–90
Painted wood, yarn
10 x 5½ x 4½″

United States
MODIFIED WING-BACK
ARMCHAIR. c. 1990
U.S. flag fabric, leather, wood,
brass tacks
11¾ x 7½ x 8½″

42

43

United States
**WINDSOR-STYLE
SWIVEL STOOL.**
20th century
Wood
10¼ x 3¾ x 3¾"

United States
**WINDSOR-STYLE
BENCH.** c. 1940–50
Wood
5 x 4¼ x 2¼"

United States
**SHAKER SLAT-BACK
CHAIR.** 1840–1910
Wood
11 x 4¾ x 4¾"

44

Above, left to right:
United States
SHAKER-STYLE SLAT-BACK ROCKER.
20th century
Wood, ribbon
9½ x 4½ x 6"

United States
SHAKER-STYLE SLAT-BACK CHAIR. 20th century
Wood, cotton
3¾ x 1¾ x 1¾"

United States
SHAKER-STYLE HIGH CHAIR. 20th century
Wood, cotton
8 x 3½ x 2¾"

Below, left to right:
United States
CANDY CANE CHAIR.
c. 1980–90
Plastic strips, rattan
5 x 4 x 4½"

United States
CLASSIC AMERICAN BISTRO CHAIR.
20th century
Twisted wire, wood
12½ x 7 x 6½"

Above, left to right:
United States
PIERCED BACK CHAIR.
Late 19th century
Wood, fringe, velvet
4½ x 1¾ x 2½"

United States
NAVAJO CHAIR. 1991
Knotted and looped twine
3½ x 2 x 2½"

United States
COUNTRY CHAIR.
19th century
Wood
4¾ x 3 x 3"

Below, left to right:
United States
**WINDSOR-STYLE SIDE
CHAIR.** 19th century
Wood
12 x 4¼ x 4"

United States
**SHEPHERD GIRL
CHAIR.** Early 20th century
Painted wood
7 x 4¼ x 4"

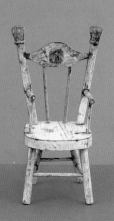

Above, left to right:

United States

DIAMOND BACK CHAIR.
20th century
Painted wood
7 x 4¼ x 4¼"

United States
PEW CHAIR. 20th century
Wood, fabric
4¼ x 4½ x 3"

Below, left to right:
United States
SPINDLE ARMCHAIR.
c. 1930
Painted wood
10¼ x 5¾ x 4¾"

United States
**COPY OF A CORNER
CHAIR.** 19th century
Painted wood
5 x 4¼ x 2¼"

The domestic nature of furniture has meant that most chairs and other seats were specifically designed for use indoors. Fine woods, delicate silk or wool fabrics, and gilded or embossed leathers, the materials most frequently used in the past for seating, restricted the geographic range of chairs to interior spaces. Furniture made specifically for outdoor use had to be made of sturdy and weather-resistant woods, impervious stone, or metal.

The world of outdoor furniture expanded greatly in the 1800s with the introduction of new materials such as cast iron, which could be easily molded into sturdy and durable garden chairs, benches, or tables. Other types of metal outdoor furniture proliferated, alongside wooden furniture made of long-lasting cedar, or treated with newly developed, often brightly colored, enamels and synthetic paints. Outdoor furniture made in miniature includes examples of both metal and wooden varieties, some in the form of suites that include benches as well as chairs. Favorites among collectors of miniature chairs are the clever and simple folding chairs from Germany, France, Italy, or the United States.

In the eighteenth century, another genre of furniture gained in popularity. So-called rustic furniture, carved to simulate the gnarled and twisted branches and roots of real trees, was planted in English parks and gardens for the delight of strollers and sitters. By the middle years of the century, designs for rustic furniture were widely circulated through engravings and pattern books.

Related to the development of this sophisticated rustic furniture were humble pieces of useful furniture made by mostly anonymous artisans of actual rough-hewn branches, twigs, and rootstocks. Rustic furniture in full scale has been made in many countries and regions, but the genre is closely identified with American provincial areas ranging from New England to the Southwest. An assortment of rustic seats has been made in miniature, ranging from spindly and spike-backed armchairs to solid and heavy loglike side chairs. Most of the pieces are made of natural, unpeeled branches, the colors of the bark serving to contrast with the pale, exposed ends of cut twigs and branches. Others are made of peeled or stained branches, and even a few in materials other than wood, as essays in trompe l'oeil ceramics.

Left to right:
Jeffrey Barnes
United States
**NAIL STOOL AND BACK-
REST.** 1992
Aluminum (unfinished), moss
8 x 2¼" (head), ½" (shaft)

Mexico
PATIO FURNITURE. 1992
Yarn, metal
Chairs: 3½ x 2 x 2¼"
Table: 6 x 4¼ x 4¼"

50

United States
TWIG CHAIR. 1990
Twigs
10 x 9 x 6″

United States
TWIG ARMCHAIR.
20th century
Twigs
11½ x 5¾ x 5½″

United States
**IMITATION TWIG
CHAIR.** c. 1930
Ceramic
7 x 4 x 4½″

52

United States
RUSTIC LOG CHAIR.
c. 1930
Wood
8¾ × 6 × 3½"

United States
TWIG ROCKER.
20th century
Twigs
12 x 4½ x 9"

United States
UNTITLED.
20th century
Twigs
12 x 7 x 7½"

United States
TWIG HEART CHAIR.
20th century
Twigs
8¼ x 4 x 5½"

53

Left to right:
France
UNTITLED. 1991
Rattan
6¼ x 3½ x 3″

Germany
UNTITLED. c. 1920
Bamboo
4 x 2½ x 2″

France
UNTITLED. 20th century
Bamboo, stenciled reed
9 x 8 x 6¾″

54

Germany
TWIG GARDEN SET.
c. 1920
Twigs
Chairs: 2½ x 1½ x 1"
Swing: 7 x 4 x 2"

France
PARK FOLDING CHAIR.
c. 1910
Wood, metal
7½ x 3 x 3"

Germany
**BIERGARTEN FOLDING
CHAIR.** Early 20th century
Steel, wood
9¼ x 6 x 6½"

Italy
FOLDING ARMCHAIR.
Early 20th century
Wood, metal
10 x 7 x 7¼"

56

United States
**LATE VICTORIAN/
EDWARDIAN ROCKER.**
c. 1920
Metal, wood
10 x 6½ x 5¾"

United States
**LATE VICTORIAN/
EDWARDIAN LOVESEAT.**
c. 1920
Metal, wood
10¼ x 11½ x 6"

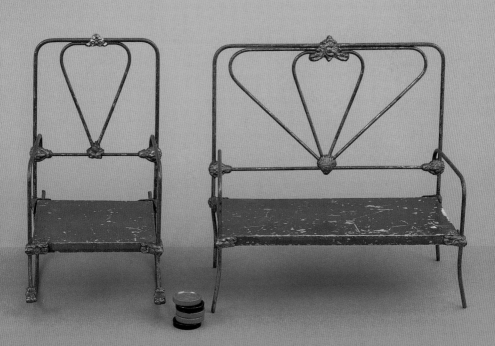

57

Left to right:
Robert Eyre
United States
LAWN CHAIR. c. 1910
Wood, ribbon
4 x 3½ x 7½″

Stomu Miyazaki
United States
**HOMAGE TO AMERICAN
DREAM.** 1986
Painted wood, Astroturf
9 x 6 x 4½″

Chair sitting on top:
Miguel Angel Morales
Mexico
SMALL STONE CHAIR.
1992
Pebbles
2½ x 1½ x 1½″

59

TRANSFORMED CHAIRS

Like lowly caterpillars that are magically transformed into glorious butterflies, miniature furniture of distinction is created by artists who transform the ordinary into the exceptional. Many of these artists focus on the ways in which materials can be transformed into forms and shapes unseen and unexpected. Some of the transformations are understandable as metaphors of function: chairs made of table cutlery, for instance, evoke memories of dining with family or friends. Other transformations give validity to the ephemera of our daily lives in chairs made of paper tickets, cigarettes and lighters, and empty bottles of chili pepper sauce, a veritable hot seat!

Clever and ingenious juxtapositions of form and function in such transformations include comforting breakfast chairs made of real bagels, or barbecue benches made of hot dog buns. Some seats made of spiky scrub brushes suggest that comfort, like beauty, may be in the eye (and posterior) of the beholder. Beer cans and tin cans, along with discarded cigarette packages, continue a lively folk-art spirit.

The idea of a chair is insepara-
bly linked to our awareness that sitting
erect and perpendicular to the ground is
both a human trait and a human aber-
ration. Some artists play on the trans-
formative idea, resulting in chairs that are close in spirit to actual
shamanistic objects. In so doing, their makers suggest that the spirit of
nature is captured in these materials; transformed chairs made of wheat
sheaves and dried flowers are poignant reminders that nature and art may be
indivisible. Other chairs, made of carefully selected beach pebbles and feathers,
echo this transformative theme.

Transformative miniature furniture is also informed by concerns that are
particularly significant today, such as recycling and the use of "green" materials,
reminding us that transformation is, in its essence, a matter of perception and
understanding that can embrace both personal visions as well as global issues.

61

Gregory Beylerian
United States
SELF-PORTRAIT (motorized wheelchair that makes noise and lights up). 1992
New York City public telephone, circuit board, phaser gun
10 x 5½ x 5¼"

Each:
Jerry Hall
United States
UNTITLED. 1992
Stainless steel and silver-
plated flatware
8½ x 3¾ x 3¾"

Anna Webjorn
Sweden
UNTITLED. 1992
Wire
9 x 2¾ x 3¼"

Jean Campbell
United States
TABASCO CHAIR. 1992
Brillo pads, tabasco sauce
bottles, rubber bands, wood
11½ x 4 x 5"

Beverly Buchanan
United States
RING CHAIR. 1992
Pine, tin, staples, abalone,
brass tacks, ring buttons, ink
4 x 2¼ x 3"

Lloyd Schwan for Godley-
Schwan
United States
WIRE ON WIRE. 1990
Wire
5¼ x 3 x 4¼"

64

Steven Buettner
United States
PUBLIC LOUNGE CHAIR.
1992
Hydrostone
3½ x 3¼ x 4¾"

Stephen W. Yemm/Yemm &
Hart Green Materials
United States
PIONEER. 1993
Recycled plastics
7 x 4½ x 4½"

John Grant
United States
LIGHTER CHAIR. 1992
Cigarettes, lighters
4 x 4½ x 3"

Left to right:
Neal Small
United States
DECK CHAIR. 1992
Playing cards
3 x 5½ x 5"

CLUB CHAIR. 1992
Playing cards
3¼ x 3 x 3½"

**COMMERCIAL CLASSIC
CHAIR—FLAME
RETARDANT.** 1991
Matchbook, paper clips
1¾ x 1½ x 2"

SPRING IS HERE. 1992
Wire spring, wood
4 x 2¼ x 1¾"

SCRUB BRUSH CHAIR.
1991
Scrub brush, wood
5 x 8 x 3¾"

**VEGETABLE BRUSH
CHAIR.** 1991
Scrub brush
5 x 6 x 3¾"

**100% WOOD CHAIR &
OTTOMAN.** 1991
Tree bark
3 x 4½ x 3"

Rick Ladd
United States
UNTITLED. 1990
Folded and woven magazine
strips, cellophane
6½ x 4½ x 3½"

Jennifer Cecere
United States
AT HOME. 1992
Lace, acrylic, fabric
5 x 3½ x 4"

United States
PRISON ART. c. 1950
Folded and woven Camel cigarette packs
9¾ x 5 x 5"

Thomas Lanigan-Schmidt
United States
CHINA EMPRESS. 1993
Chenille stems, staples, cello-
phane, gold and silver foil
5¾ x 3¼ x 2½"

PILTDOWN CHAIR. 1991
Prehistoric rocks
3 x 2½ x 2"

FLINTSTONE LOUNGE CHAIR. 1991
Pebbles, pigeon feathers
4 x 5 x 4"

MADRID ADJUSTABLE LOUNGE CHAIR. 1991
Pebbles
3 x 2½ x 2"

BEACH CHAIR #2. 1991
Painted pebbles
2 x 2 x 1¾"

70

Hervé Gambs
France
CHAISE VEGETALE. 1992
Wheat, dried roses
8½ x 5½ x 4½″

71

SCOTCH BRITE™
SCOURING PAD CHAIR.
1991
Scrub pad
4 x 3¾ x 3″

HEINEKEN BEER
STOOL. 1991
Bottle cap, wood
1½ x 1 x 1″

BAGEL CHAIR. 1991
Bagel
2 x 3½ x 3¼″

HOT DOG COUCH. 1991
Hot dog bun, wood
2¾ x 4¼ x 2¼″

DENTIST CHAIR. 1993
Plastic, teeth
¾ x 1 x 1″

Left to right:

Dominican Republic
STACKING CHAIR.
20th century
Cut and shaped tin can
4¾ x 3½ x 3″

United States
UNTITLED. 20th century
Cut and shaped beer can
3½ x 2¼ x 2½″

Aran for Handicap Sport
Association
Lebanon (b. Armenia)
UNTITLED. 1992
Cut and shaped tin can
4¾ x 2½ x 2¾″

United States
CARTOUCHE-SHAPED
SOFA. 20th century
Cut and shaped beer can
3½ x 6½ x 2½″

Russia
PIN CUSHION CHAIR.
1990
Cut and shaped tin can
4 x 3½ x 3½″

73

Josette Urso
United States
LULU. 1992
Mixed metals, copper rivets,
glass beads
4½ x 2⅝ x 3"

74

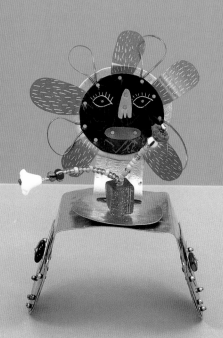

David Perry
United States
FARE CHAIR. 1992
Woven ticket stubs, wood
frame
7¾ x 4 x 4"

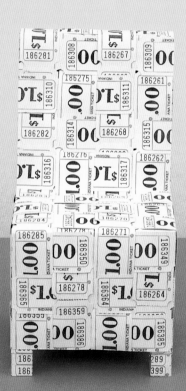

Constantin Boym for
Beylerian
United States
FANTASY PEG CHAIR.
1993
Wood frame with various
wooden chair attachments
9¼ x 4½ x 9¼″

76

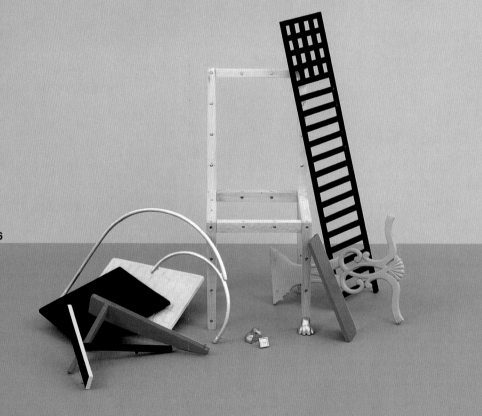

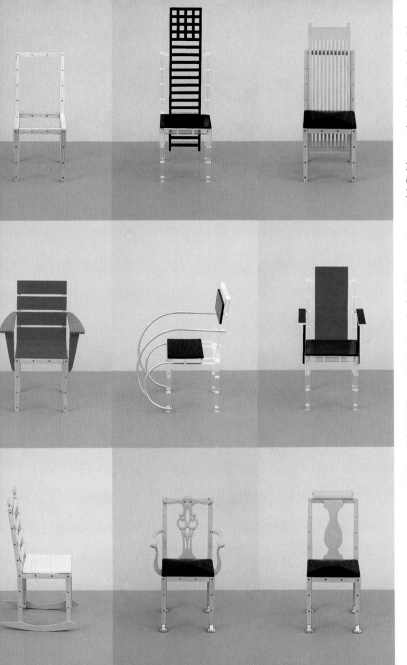

FANTASY PEG CHAIRS

WOOD FRAME. 1993
Wood
9¼ x 4½ x 4¼"

MACKINTOSH CHAIR.
1993
Wood, plastic
12¾ x 4½ x 4¼"

**FRANK LLOYD WRIGHT
CHAIR.** 1993
Painted wood
10¾ x 4½ x 4¼"

ADIRONDACK CHAIR. 1993
Painted wood
9¼ x 6 x 4¼"

**MIES VAN DER ROHE
CHAIR.** 1993
Wood, plastic
9¼ x 4½ x 6½"

**GERRIT RIETVELD
CHAIR.** 1993
Painted wood, plastic
10¼ x 5½ x 4¼"

**SLAT-BACK SHAKER
ROCKER.** 1993
Painted wood
9½ x 4½ x 4¼"

CHIPPENDALE CHAIR. 1993
Painted wood
9¼ x 5½ x 4¼"

VICTORIAN CHAIR. 1993
Painted wood
9¾ x 4½ x 4¼"

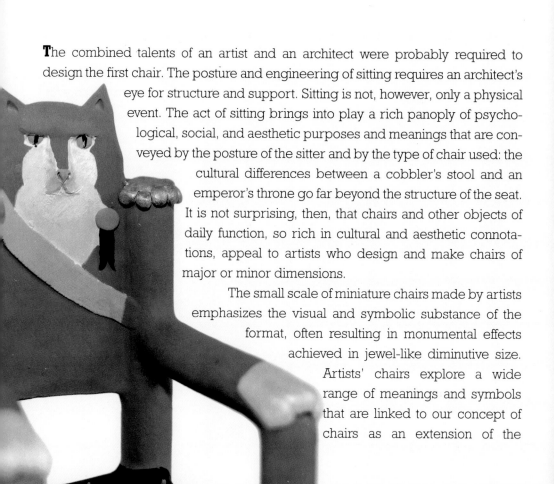

The combined talents of an artist and an architect were probably required to design the first chair. The posture and engineering of sitting requires an architect's eye for structure and support. Sitting is not, however, only a physical event. The act of sitting brings into play a rich panoply of psychological, social, and aesthetic purposes and meanings that are conveyed by the posture of the sitter and by the type of chair used: the cultural differences between a cobbler's stool and an emperor's throne go far beyond the structure of the seat. It is not surprising, then, that chairs and other objects of daily function, so rich in cultural and aesthetic connotations, appeal to artists who design and make chairs of major or minor dimensions.

The small scale of miniature chairs made by artists emphasizes the visual and symbolic substance of the format, often resulting in monumental effects achieved in jewel-like diminutive size.

Artists' chairs explore a wide range of meanings and symbols that are linked to our concept of chairs as an extension of the human body. Rarely do they refer to standard or ordinary forms; through juxtaposition of often surprising or provocative images or symbols, and by using the format of the chair as a matrix for associative or connotative meanings, artists remind us that chairs are significant elements in the theater of daily life.

Some artists have achieved these effects through the use of techniques such as collage, in which disparate elements are brought together within the structure of the chair, or are applied to the surfaces as flat patterns or textures made of glass jewels and beads, shattered mirrors, or paper. Some chairs are explorations of pure shape, form, color, and texture. Other innovators have used wire to create densely woven and wrapped structures or, by contrast, light and air-filled calligraphic "drawings" of chairs in three dimensions.

79

Artists have drawn upon the rich history of ritual furniture, creating thrones for the imaginary royalty of one's dreams. Some chairs evoke the distant and archetypal world of prehistory. Others take on forms generally associated with reliquaries or funereal monuments. The psychological dimension of sitting is suggested in many artists' chairs by combining ordinary chairs with extraordinary elements like flying fish, human hands, fruit, flowers, or even fungi. Far and beyond the richest resource for designers of these chairs is the world of nature, ranging from animals to landscapes, from the innocence of twigs and moss to the veiled threats of thorny branches.

Left to right:
Douglas Fitch
United States
DREAM CHAIR. 1992
Polyester resin, polyurethane
foam, brass rod
9 x 6 x 5½″

Michele Oka Doner
United States
TERRIBLE CHAIR. 1991
Bronze
5½ x 3 x 2½″

80

81

Gregory Beylerian
United States
Left:
FATHER'S DAY GIFT.
1989
Fimo®, copper, blades
7 x 3¾ x 5¼"

Right:
FATHER'S DAY GIFT.
1990
Clay, mirror pieces
6¾ x 3¾ x 5"

82

Tanya Hovnanian
United States
JEWELS. 1991
Forged steel

Left:
9½ x 4 x 4½"

Right:
7½ x 3¼ x 3"

83

Jon Brooks
United States
**STYX LADDERBACK
CHAIR.** 1992
Maple, acrylic, lacquer,
mahogany base
12½ x 2 x 2″

84

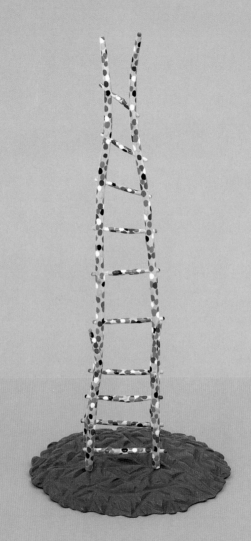

Stephen Huneck
United States
**VERMONT RAINBOW
CHAIR.** 1992
Painted basswood
12 x 8 x 5″

85

Tara K. Daly
United States
UNTITLED. 1992
Wire, electrical tape,
photographs
Left to right:
9 x 2 x 3″
9 x 5 x 4″
10 x 3 x 4½″

86

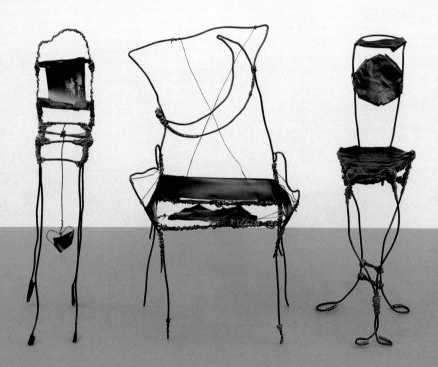

Ries Niemi
United States
UNTITLED. 1991
Metal
8¾ x 5¾ x 5″

Paul Suttman
United States
BRAQUE'S CHAIR. 1992
Bronze
11¾ x 4¼ x 4¼″

Rob Szabo
United States
THE CHAIR. 1989
Metal
9 x 5 x 5″

87

Solveig Cox
United States

GENERAL CHAIR. 1991
Painted ceramic
12 x 6 x 5½"

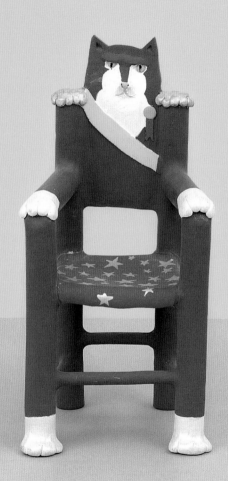

Maynard Hale Lyndon
United States
Left to right:
TOAD STOOL. 1991
Wood, plated brass
9½ x 6½ x 6½"

PAIR PEAR CHAIR. 1991
Aniline-dyed hardwood pears
with pine seat
7¼ x 6½ x 6½"

89

Mike & Debbie
Schramer/Whimsical Twigs
United States
THE GAZEBO CHAIR.
1992
Birch branches, grapevine
tendrils, moss, roses, pods,
herb leaves
7 x 6 x 3½"

90

Cheryl R. Riley
United States
**CHAIR FOR A
RENAISSANCE QUEEN.**
1992
Glass, iron, steel, copper
12½ x 3½ x 3½"

91

Robert Ebendorf
United States
Left:
CROSS CHAIR. 1992
Wood, pencils, glass, paper,
metal
9 x 3½ x 3½"

Right:
LFT. ADOLPH PINQUE.
1992
Wood, glass, paper, metal,
painting reproduction
8½ x 3 x 4"

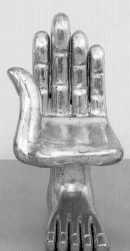

Pedro Friedeberg
Mexico
Left to right:
BUTTERFLY CHAIR. 1991
(original design 1962)
Gold leaf, paint, wood
6½ x 3½ x 3¾"

**MODEL FOR LIFE-SIZE
HAND CHAIR.** 1991
(original design 1962)
Gold leaf, wood
5¼ x 3 x 3¼"

**MODEL FOR LIFE-SIZE
HAND CHAIR.** 1991
(original design 1962)
Gold leaf, wood
4 x 2½ x 3"

93

Paul Von Ringleheim
United States
CONSTELLATION. c. 1992
Steel wire, painted wood
5 x 2½ x 2¼″

Mexico
FATSO CHAIR. 1992
Painted wood
6¼ x 7 x 5¾″

Nancy Friedmann
United States
ROSEY ARMCHAIR. 1991
Papier-maché
4 x 4 x 3″

Mexico
CROCHET CHAIR. 1991
Yarn, metal
7½ x 5 x 4½″

94

Szu-Min Kuo
Korea
UNTITLED. 1992
Ceramic
9 x 3 x 3″

Robert Arko
United States
1981 STUDY MODEL.
1981
Wood, steel rod, paint
11 x 4 x 5″

Kyung Soo Yim
Korea
THE WISH CHAIR. 1987
Copper, silk
9 x 3 x 3½″

Ayse Birsel
United States (b. Turkey)
THE EVIL-EYE CHAIR.
1993
Wood tool handles, twine,
Turkish evil-eye bead
10 x 4 x 4½″

Michael Wolk
United States
TROPICAL SLAT CHAIR.
1993
Basswood
6¾ x 5 x 6⅝″

Hervé Gambs
France
CHAISE VEGETALE. 1992
Wood, dried roses, bronze
10 x 4½ x 4½″

Jake Steinberg
United States
UNTITLED. 1991
Painted wood
6 x 3¼ x 3½"

Pat Tillery, Robert Coates,
Abigail Reponen, Robert
Rabinowitz
United States
BIRTHDAY CHAIR. 1991
Collage over Styrofoam
9¾ x 6¼ x 5½"

Jon Schooler
Mexico (b. United States)
IDA'S CHAIR. 1992
Handmade paper
5 x 3¼ x 2½"

Left to right:
Dana Wechselbaum
United States
ATTIC CHAIR. 1992
Wood, metal beads
7½ x 3½ x 3¼″

Carina Beylerian
United States
HULA CHAIR. 1992
Wood, metal beads
7½ x 3½ x 3¼″

Margo Tantau Kearney
United States
BISTRO CHAIR. 1992
Galvanized wire
5¾ x 3 x 3″

Pamela Fritz
United States
POM-POM CHAIR. 1992
Metal, fringe, crushed velvet
11½ x 4½ x 4″

Margo Tantau Kearney
United States
TRIANGLE CHAIR. 1992
Galvanized wire
5¼ x 3¼ x 3¼″

Left to right:

Mexico
**UNTITLED HUICHOL
CHAIR.** 1992
Glass beads, wood
9 x 4½ x 5"

Hu Hung-shu
United States
**ONE OF THE STEP-
SETTERS.** 1981
Painted wood board
22½ x 12 x 33"

Terry Rosenberg
United States
ANTALYA ROCKER. 1991
Polyethylene
6½ x 6 x 6½"

101

Lloyd Schwan for Godley-
Schwan
United States
Left:
TWISTED WIRE. 1990
Brass wire, felt
5¼ x 3 x 4½″

Right:
CARTOON. 1990
Brass wire, felt
4¾ x 5 x 3½″

102

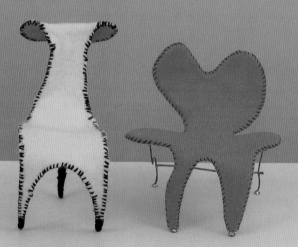

Sylvia Netzer
United States
Left:
**WILDER GARDEN
CHAIR.** 1993
Ceramic
6¾ x 3½ x 4″

Right:
GARDEN CHAIR. 1993
Ceramic
5⅛ x 3¼ x 3¼″

103

Carol Sarkisian
United States
ARTIST CHAIR. 1993
Wood, glass beads, freshwater
pearls, Swarovski crystals,
rhinestones
4 x 3¼ x 2¾″

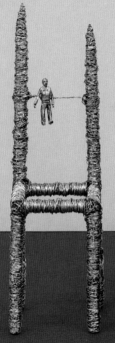

Left:
Melissa Stern
United States
TIGHTROPE CHAIR. 1992
Wood, steel, wire, lead
7 x 3 x 3½"

Right:
© Nina Yankowitz
United States
BOUFFANTE CHAIR. 1992
Coated magnet wire
5½ x 3 x 3"

106

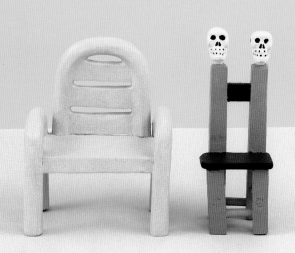

Left to right:
Angelico Jimenez
Mexico
UNTITLED. 1991
Painted wood
9½ x 5½ x 7½"

Pedro Ramirez
Mexico
UNTITLED. 1991
Painted wood
7¾ x 5½ x 4"

Achihuatzin
Mexico
UNTITLED. 1992
Painted ceramic
6 x 2 x 2"

Bali
UNTITLED. 1992
Painted wood
7 x 5½ x 3½"

Pedro Rodriguez
Mexico
**LOS DIAS DE LOS
MUERTOS (DAY OF THE
DEAD).** 1992
Painted wood
8 x 3 x 2½"

Mexico
SEMANA SANTA CEREMONIAL CHAIR.
20th century
Hand-carved wood chair
9½ x 4½ x 4"

United States
TRAMP ART. 20th century
Wood, photograph, glass
7¼ x 5½ x 4"

108

United States
**CROWN THORN TRAMP
ART.** 20th century
Wood
6 x 3¼ x 2½"

Peter Stamberg
United States
**CARDINAL DOTTS
CHAIR.** 1978
Wood
6½ x 2½ x 2"

United Kingdom
UNTITLED. c. 1850–1914
Glass beads, wire, wood
5 x 3 x 3½"

109

Left to right:
Hermone Futrell
United States
RUSTIC CHAIR. 1993
Sugar maple
9 x 2½ x 2"

Indonesia
UNTITLED. 1991
Painted wood
5½ x 2½ x 1¾"

Mexico
UNTITLED. 1991
Painted wood
7½ x 2¾ x 2½"

Italy
UNTITLED. c. 1930
Painted wood
8½ x 4¾ x 4"

111

Canan Tolon
United States
SEATABLE (seat folds to
form table). 1989
Sheet metal
6¾ x 7 x 3¼″

Robert M. Stewart
United States
WIRED CHAIR. 1992
Steel tube, neoprene rubber
3 x 4 x 4″

Jordan Steckel
United States
**COMPUTER CHIP
CHAIR.** 1988
Caster, plaster
10½ x 3 x 3½″

112

Frederic Schwartz
United States
HOUSE CHAIR. 1992
Ceramic
5⅝ x 4½ x 2½"

Kjell Engman, produced at
Kosta Boda Atelier
Sweden
BONBON CHAIR. 1992
Glass
2¾ x 3½ x 3"

Scott Richard Brazeau
United States
DYSLEXIA CHAIR. 1993
Steel
10⅛ x 4½ x 4¼"

David D'Imperio
United States
CUMULUS CHAIR. 1992
Cellulose acetate, wood,
enamel
4½ x 2½ x 3½"

113

Toward the end of the seventeenth century, furniture design
changed dramatically as a result of the growing use of fabrics and
upholstery to make chairs more beautiful and certainly more comfortable. Chairs had always served practical purposes of work and
leisure. Status and wealth were embodied by elegant chairs that dis-
played elaborate craftsmanship in the carving or painting, or in their use of
rare and expensive materials. *Comfort* as a major concern, however, is a late
arrival to the world of furniture design. Upholstered furniture, fitted with cush-
ions or covered in padded fabrics, began to appear more frequently in the
1600s. By the eighteenth century, easy chairs were expected accoutrements in
well-appointed drawing rooms—comfortably padded and
capacious, these seats were welcoming havens for the
world-weary and foot fatigued. In the nineteenth century,
the invention of the coiled metal spring further enhanced
the comfort level of seating. Variations on comfortable
padded chairs were seemingly unlimited: slipper chairs, loung-
ing chairs, wing chairs, club chairs and, of course, rocking chairs. An
extraordinary portrait of this family of chairs has been left to posterity by makers
of miniature chairs.

In *The Rocking Chair Book,* authors Peter and Ellen Denker mention an
1844 Vermont newspaper notice calling rocking chairs "wooden narcotics." The
hypnotic comforts of this particular form of chair have been appreciated for gen-

erations since the eighteenth century. The innovative design of a rocking chair, which features curved rails that link front and back legs at each side, may have had something to do with rocking horses used by small children in seventeenth-century English and German homes. By the nineteenth century, the rocking chair had become ubiquitous in American homes, where it has always found a special place in both full-scale and miniature versions.

The comfort and pleasure of being gently rocked back and forth in a rocking chair was not always deemed appropriate for everyone. While children and the elderly were considered special cases in need of such solace, rocking chairs were thought by some to be inappropriate for healthy adults. Today, the rocking chair is a truly democratic design: mothers rock their children to sleep in them, elderly individuals doze in them, and poets and even presidents work in them. To everyone's delight, the genre has not been overlooked by makers of miniature furniture, whose works range from realistic scaled-down versions of specific types of rockers—Shaker, Adirondack, or wicker—to fantastic assemblages made of horseshoes and lace, or of deconstructed clothespins.

Asia
CHANDERNAGOR. 1993
Wood, cane
8 x 6¼ x 6"

116

Left:
Richard Bennett
United States
THE CAT SEAT. 1993
Leather, aluminum, wood
4½ x 9¾ x 4½"

Right:
United States
**UPHOLSTERED
ARMCHAIR.** c. 1930
Velvet, wood
4 x 3¾ x 3½"

117

Left to right:
United States
VICTORIAN ROCKER.
Late 19th century
Simulated bamboo
5 x 4¼ x 5″

United States
LOUNGE CHAIR. c. 1950
Fabric, wood
8¼ x 8¼ x 9″

France
ART DECO CHAIR.
c. 1930–40
Fabric, wood
4½ x 3 x 3½″

119

United States
HORSESHOE ROCKER.
c. 1930
Metal horseshoes, string
7½ x 5¼ x 5½"

Spain
TOY CHAIR. c. 1950
Lithographed tinplate
6 x 2½ x 5½"

United States
PONY SHOE ROCKER.
20th century
Metal pony shoes, lace fabric
5¼ x 3½ x 4½"

United States
UNTITLED. c. 1920
Wood
5½ x 2½ x 3¼"

120

United States
CLOTHESPIN CHAIR.
1992
Clothespins
5 x 3¼ x 5"

United States
CAT ROCKING CHAIR.
c. 1920
Painted wood
9¾ x 6¼ x 9¼"

United States
WOVEN ROCKER.
20th century
Wood
8 x 6 x 10½"

121

"I had three chairs in my house: one for solitude, two for friendship, three for society," wrote Henry David Thoreau. For a collector of miniature chairs, such asceticism would be difficult, if not impossible, to defend.

The history of miniature chairs expresses the dreams and visions of artists, the material and physical knowledge of engineers, and the cultural and artistic purview of historians. This genre of artifact follows closely the myriad developments in technology, as well as the perennial shifts in taste and fashion that describe the world of furniture and design history. Miniature versions of chairs that have become landmarks in the history of design, or that epitomize a stylistic phenomenon, are prized among collectors.

The grown-up world of antique collectors has a parallel in miniature chairs, the designs of which evoke the world of eighteenth-century Neoclassicism as viewed by Hepplewhite and Sheraton. Nineteenth-century tastes in furniture design are also recorded in the chinoiserie designs based on exotic bamboo furniture, or in those designs which respond to the technology of bentwood, popularized by innovators like Thonet.

Design classics of early Modernism have also proliferated in the world of miniature furniture, and it is now possible to own examples of rare designs like the attenuated geometric furniture of Charles Rennie Mackintosh, or the supremely refined designs of Josef Hoffmann. Even the famous bent tubular steel chair designed by Marcel Breuer has been transformed into a miniature, joining other "classics" by Gerrit Rietveld of Holland and Hans Wegner of Denmark.

These design classics extend the idea of miniaturization from the world of antiques and history right into the living rooms and dining rooms of contemporary life. As artifacts, these miniature seats offer an unusually pleasurable way of retelling our past. As works of imagination, craftsmanship, and passion, they may also inspire our fantasies and dreams of the future.

ARTS & CRAFTS STYLE.
Early 20th century
Painted wood
7½ x 3½ x 3¼"

SCANDINAVIAN STYLE.
Early 20th century
Painted wood
7¼ x 3 x 3¼"

CANADIAN SIDE CHAIR.
Early 20th century
Painted wood
6½ x 2½ x 2½"

**PIERCED-BACK
ITALIANATE STYLE.**
19th century
Painted wood
6½ x 3¼ x 3¼"

124

Josef Hoffmann
CABARET FLEDERMAUS.
1907
Reproduced by Galerie
Ambiente Miniatur
Painted wood
4¾ x 3½ x 3″

Josef Hoffmann
SITZMASCHINE. 1905
Reproduced by Galerie
Ambiente Miniatur
Painted wood
7 x 4 x 5½″

Gerrit Rietveld
**ROODBLAUWE STOEL
(RED AND BLUE
CHAIR).** 1918
Painted wood
5¾ x 3¾ x 5¼″

Charles Mackintosh
HILL HOUSE. 1903
Fabric, aluminum
11 x 3¼ x 2⅞″

125

Hans J. Wegner
PEACOCK. 1947
Reproduced by Yoshikazy
Hamada
Wood, cord
8¼ x 6 x 4¼"

Marcel Breuer
WASSILY. 1925
Reproduced by Modell & Form
Metal, leather
6 x 6¼ x 5"

ART DECO STYLE.
c. 1930
Metal, leather
4 x 4¾ x 3"

126

Above, left to right:
Ludwig Mies van der Rohe
MR. 1926. Metal, 2¼ x 1¼ x 2"

Michele de Lucchi
FIRST. 1983. Metal, 2½ x 2 x 1"

Charles & Ray Eames
DCWL 1946. Metal, 2¼ x 1½ x 1¾"
Each reproduced by ACME studios

CHARLES X STYLE.
Early 19th century
Wood, fabric
9 x 4½ x 4¼"

HEPPLEWHITE STYLE.
1790–1810
Painted wood, fabric
6¾ x 3¼ x 3"

SHERATON STYLE.
1790–1810
Painted wood, fabric
6 x 3¼ x 2¾"

**TURNED AND CARVED
STYLE.** 17th century
Painted wood
6½ x 3¼ x 3¼"

127

**THONET-STYLE SIDE
CHAIR.** 19th century
Wood
6¾ x 3 x 3"

**THONET-STYLE
ARMCHAIR.** 19th century
Wood
7 x 4¼ x 3½"

**VICTORIAN BAMBOO
DESIGN.** Late 19th century
Bamboo
10 x 6 x 4"

128

BAUHAUS STYLE. 1930
Metal, fabric
5 x 3½ x 3″

Charles & Ray Eames
RAR. 1950
Reproduced by Vitra Design
Museum
Plastic, wood, metal
4½ x 4 x 4½″

KITCHEN CHAIR. c. 1950
Painted metal
3 x 2¼ x 2½″

Achille and Pier Giacomo
Castiglioni
SANLUCA. 1960
Reproduced by Bernini
Plastic
6¾ x 4¾ x 5″

The history of the chair as we know it today—a seat equipped with a back and arms—cannot be separated from the history of power and status. The chair form was derived from ancient thrones, the use of which was restricted to the most powerful echelon of ancient societies. Thrones for rulers are known as early as the Babylonian period, but it was the Egyptians who may have made some of the first true chairs. And while chairs are known to have existed in some quantity in Greece and Rome, they were still limited in numbers and use to those of high status; some ancient Roman grave markers even show the deceased sitting in a favorite chair.

It was not until as recently as the seventeenth century that chairs began to appear in numbers large enough to suggest that they were being adopted for use by broader segments of the population. Although we have lost touch with many historical meanings of chairs, we need only remember that dining room sets today are still generally made with two *arm*chairs and varying numbers of *armless* chairs to suggest status differences between those who sit at the "heads" of tables.

Through their distinctive forms and decorations, makers of miniature chairs remind us of the many cultural and historical connotations of seats of power. Some chairs recall the unlimited powers of ancient rulers such as King Tut, whose popularity today has made him one of the "superstars" of the ancient world. Other chairs seen here evoke the elegant world of Napoleon's powerful and far-flung empire, or that of his nemesis, the Duke of Wellington!

In addition to confirming status, chairs can also convey information about roles and occupations through association. For example, ambiguity can be detected in the complex relationship between sitter and stylist in a barber's chair, in which the high-status sitter is required to take a posture of subservience at the hand of the barber. And few will deny the powerful status of the lifeguard, whose elevated chair facilitates vision and reassures bathers. Unlimited power and control are suggested in images of chairs of execution, their clinical appearance underlining their sinister purpose. At the other end of the spectrum is the personal seat of power in our bathrooms, from which a sitter truly rules all he or she surveys.

United States
**LIFEGUARD CHAIR
WITH INITIALS JAE.**
20th century
Painted metal
5½ x 6¼ x 4"

132

Bruce and Chloé Simoneaux
United States

THRONES OF LILLIPUT.
1993
Lego Blocks
Left:
9 x 5 x 3"
Right:
7½ x 3⅛ x 2½"

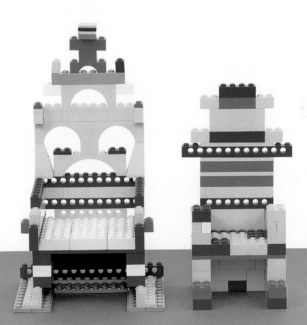

133

United States
BARBER'S CHAIR. 1991
Ceramic
6 x 3¼ x 4″

Right:
Japan
TOILET. 1991
Porcelain
5 x 3 x 4¼″

134

Theatrical Creations, Inc.
United States
**PROMOTION FOR THE
KING TUTANKHAMEN
EXHIBITION** (box). 1978
Gold leaf over resin
7 x 4 x 5″

Spain
DUKE OF WELLINGTON CHAIR. Late 19th–early 20th century
A model of one of a set of chairs presented to the Duke of Wellington by Spain
Wood, leather, Wellington Crest seal
7 x 3½ x 3½″

France
HIGH-BACK CHAIR.
c. 19th century
Wood
9½ x 4¾ x 4″

France
THRONE CHAIR. c. 1920
Decoupage wood
11 x 6 x 5¼″

136

France
EMPIRE-STYLE CHAIR.
c. 1803—19
Wood, fabric
9¼ x 7 x 6″

United States
**KING TUTANKHAMEN
THRONE.** 20th century
Bronze
7¾ x 5 x 4½″

China
PALACE CHAIR (one of a
pair). Early 19th century
Wood, gold paint detailing
5 x 3½ x 2½″

137

United States
P.O.W. CHAIR. 1917
Wooden puzzle pieces
12½ x 6½ x 6½″

138

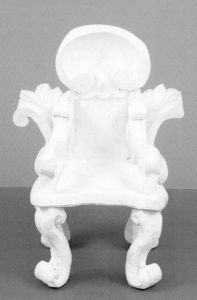

Produced by Neidermaier
United States
**MINIATURE CROWN
CHAIR ("DOROTHY'S
THRONE").** 1985
Display Chair for Neidermaier
Fiberglass resin
8 x 5 x 4″

139

Andrea Branzi
Italy
HOMAGE NOGUCHI. 1993
Wood, plaster, Plexiglas,
branch
16 x 21¾ x 6¼"

140

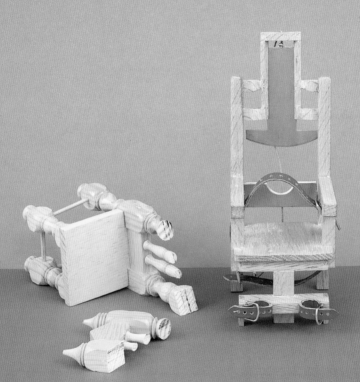

Dragoslav Scepanovic
United States (b. Yugoslavia)
THE END (OLD SPARKY)
(view shows chair beheaded
by guillotine). 1993
Oak, steel guillotine
10 x 4 x 4½"

141

ACKNOWLEDGMENTS

The author wishes to thank all the artists and friends who made this collection possible:

Achihvatzin
Agid, Nick
Agostino, Ed and Sylvia
Allan, Edward, Mary &
  Jennifer
Amini, Massoud
Arko, Robert
Armitage, Marsha
Arvisu, Dan
Bachelier, Violaine
Barnes, Jeffrey
Bauer, Dorothy
Bennett, Richard
Beylerian, Carina
Beylerian, Gregory
Beylerian, Louise
Birsel, Ayse Gul
Boym, Constantin
Brazeau, Scott
Brooks, Jon
Broquant, Judith
Buchanan, Beverly
Buche, Sonia
Buettner, Steven
Cameron, Elsa
Campbell, Jean
Caniato, Michele
Castelli Ferrieri, Anna
Cecere, Jennifer
The Chicago Atheneum
Coates, Robert
Cox, Solveig
Daly, Tara
D'Imperio, David

Donahue, Debra
Dudley, Lorry Parks
Dufresne, Polly
Durand, Bertram
Eames, Robert
Ebendorf, Robert
Edwards, Ethel
Eyre, Robert
Farland, Evelyn
Feldman, Janice
Fernandez, Carlos
Fitch, Douglas
Fleisher, Sidney
Friedeberg, Pedro
Friedemann, Nancy
Fritz, Pamela
Fuess, Elaine
Futrell, Hermone
Gallery of Functional Arts,
  Lois Lambert
Galloway, Cameron
Gambs, Hervé
Ganjian, Linda
Gillman, Barbara
Globus, Dorothy
Godley, Lynn
Goganian, Aida and Armenag
Gottwald, Laura
Grant, John
Gresham, David
Hall, Jerry
Hansen, J.
Hastrich, James
Heinz, Jo

Hinrichs, Bruce
Hovnanian, Tanya
Hovnanian, Nina
Hu, Hung-shu
Huneck, Stephen
Italcomma S.R.L.
Jain, Shailendra Pratap
Jiminez, Angelico
Kagan, Larry
Kahn, Jenette
Kisak, Kris
Kalins, Dorothy
Kaplan, Jacques
Karalias, Iannis
Kearney, Margo Tantau
Kirikian, Richard
Kiviat, Stephen
Krens, Thomas
Kuo, Szu-Min
Kuony, Liane
La Furlana
Ladd, Rick
Laine, Christian
Lange, Gerd and Renate
Lanigan-Schmidt, Thomas
Levi-Smith, Jackson
Lillejord, John
Lopata, Sam
Lyndon, Lu and Maynard
Lyons, Susan
Melchor, Innocencio Vazques
Melikyan, Sevan
Melrose, Clark
Milne, Victoria

Miyazaki, Stomu
Morales, Miguel Angel
Morello, Antonio
Mourgue, Pascal
Muenzer, Fred and Terry
Musto, Adam
Netzer, Sylvia
Niemi, Ries
Oka Doner, Michele
Panton, Verner
Pensoy, Barbara
Perry, David
Phagan, Patricia
Rabinowitz, Robert
Ramirez, Pedro
Reif, Rita
Reponen, Abigail
Riley, Cheryl
Rodriguez, Pedro
Rosenberg, Terry
Ruggles, Kay
Ryniewski, Glen
Saltzman, Ralph
Sarkisian, Carol
Sasson, Zimmie
Savoie, Donato
Scepanovic, Dragoslav
Schooler, Jon and Karen
Schramer, Mike and Debbie
Schramm, Pegge
Schwan, Lloyd
Schwartz, Frederic
Simoneaux, Bruce
Simoneaux, Chloé
Small, Neal
Solish, Dhana

Spiegel, Len
Staffelbach, Andre
Stamberg, Peter
Steckel, Jordan
Steigenwall, John
Steinberg, Jake
Stern, Melissa
Stewart, Robert M.
Stow Davis Furniture
Suttman, Paul
Szabo, Rob
Tanier, George
Tegnazian, Dorothy
Tillery, Pat
Tolon, Canan
Tutunjian, Lucy
Urso, Josette
Vitra Museum, Alexander Von
  Vegesack
Von Ringleheim, Paul
Wallack, Pierre
Warlamis, Heidi
Weatherend Estate Furniture
Webjorn, Anna
Wechselbaum, Dana
Wegner, Hans
Wines, James
Winter, Sandra
Wolk, Michael
Yankelovich, Hasmig
Yankowitz, Nina
Yemm and Hart
Yim, Kyung Soo
Yoshikazu, Hamada
Zadourian, Mike and Annie
Zimmermann, Marlene

Chairmania Advisors:
Emilio Ambasz
Andrea Branzi
Giulio Castelli
Luc d'Iberville-Moreau
Milton Glaser
David McFadden

143